Contents

Copyright Page
Dedication
Introduction

CHAPTER ONE
Dream

CHAPTER TWO
Vision

CHAPTER THREE
Goals

CHAPTER FOUR
Plan

CHAPTER FIVE
Conclusion

Life is what you make it

Introduction

Too often we hear expressions like, "Dare to dream!", "Dream big!", "Dream the impossible!" and "May your dreams come true!" I'm an advocate of positive expressions and I certainly appreciate people sharing them with me. My only issue, there was nothing to attach my dreams to current reality. If I took the expressions and left them at that, all I would have is the dream itself. Dreams by themselves are awesome! In our slumber we get to be anything, do anything, have anything; nothing is impossible, but when we wake up to live our lives do we put ourselves in the position to accomplish the dreams we had the night before? Do we know how?

We often place emphasis on wanting our dreams to come true. We must emphasize how to make our dreams come true as well. Desire is only a fraction of the equation for what is required to realize our dreams. If we don't learn how to make our dreams real, we will be frustrated and eventually defeated. Knowledge is critical to navigate through life

Simon Billy Bleuh Flake

BLEUHDREAM PUBLISHING
NEW JERSEY
Copyright © 2015 by Simon Billy Bleuh Flake

Edited by Simon Billy Bleuh Flake

Cover design: Masterpiece Design Group

Twitter: @billybleuh

Email: bleuhdream@gmail.com

ISBN 978-0-9969520-1-9

Dedication

I thank God for still being in the dream distribution business. I dedicate this book to my lovely wife, Whitney, our children, and all of the dreamers who put this into practice. Don't ever be discouraged by life's challenges, circumstances, or haters, none of them can stop you!

successfully. People are destroyed for lack of knowledge.[1] In essence, we perish for what we don't know or for what we know and won't practice. Our dreams are not exempt from this principle. If we don't know how to realize our dreams or know how to realize them and refuse to take the proper steps to make them real, our dreams will perish as well.

Dreams don't just come to fruition by chance or luck, they are deliberately realized by concerting visions, goals, and plans mixed with dedicated hard work and consistent effort. With no vision (cultivated dream), goals (objectives that lead us to accomplish the vision), and plan (method to achieve our goals) we have no connection to the reality in which we live and the dream we wish for. My purpose is to assist you in connecting your present, to the dreams you aspire to achieve in your future. I hypothesize if I provide you, the Dreamer, with the tools and paradigms necessary to capture your dream, envision your desired future,

---

[1] biblegateway,"" biblegateway.com, accessed October 21, 2015, https://www.biblegateway.com/passage/?search=hosea+4%3A6&version=KJV.

establish clear significant goals, and plan to achieve them, then you will be able to not only connect to your future by deliberately practicing these principles daily, but also bring others along with you and teach them as you go. You will discover dreams are not farfetched figments of the mythical mind but:

Deliberately Realized Ends Achieved Methodically© (D.R.E.A.M.).

Let's do this!

CHAPTER ONE

Dreams

"Hope deferred makes the heart sick, but a dream fulfilled is a tree of life"[2]

At one point in life all things were possible and there was no limit to our imagination, potential, or hope in our heart. Nothing could deter nor discourage us from accomplishing what we saw when we closed our eyes and imagined the infinite possibilities that awaited us in our future. Once we grew older and experienced our share of disappointments we started to minimize our dreams. As life's programming settled into our soul, our dreams got smaller by the year, to the extent they have become insignificant or non-existent. Everyday life became too cumbersome. Wishful

---

[2] biblegateway,"" biblegateway.com, accessed October 21, 2015,
https://www.biblegateway.com/passage/?search=proverbs+13%3A12&version=NLT

thinking and inflation imposed their will on the price and value of what we allowed ourselves to imagine. It seemed as if we got to a certain place where we intentionally made dreaming illegal to protect ourselves from the heartbreak of another disappointment.

Though we made this agreement with ourselves, we're still in the fight. A spark of hope compelled us to rekindle a flame that when fueled with this philosophy and practice will burn in the midst of icy adversity and the circumstances set against us will not be able to extinguish it.

In this chapter we will define dream, discuss where it comes from, and shed light upon the importance of capturing it prior to its departure. Congratulations! You have taken the first step to deliberately realizing ends (your dream) achieved methodically. With a little flicker of hope you dare to try again, and with the small event you set in motion, you will perpetuate a conflagration hot enough to burn obstacles like popsicles on a hot open flame.

Dream is a noun defined as a succession of images, thoughts, or emotions passing through the mind during sleep.[3] Dreams are usually abstract and fleeting. They can be weird at times and difficult to interpret. If you're lucky, you may be able to remember a full dream or capture the main idea as you're awakened by your alarm. Dreams come from God. Throughout biblical texts, dreams were one way God communicated with people. Though times have changed considerably, God has not, He is still in the business of guiding lives via dreams. Though dreams come from Him, it is important for us to understand, we must provide the required human action to bring them to pass. There is no substitute for human effort.

We spend every waking moment inundated with the concerns of our busy conscious life, distracted from His intention for us by what we perceive with our senses. Though He makes several attempts to get us to notice Him in our conscious state, we manage to miss

---

[3] dictionary,"" dictionary.com, accessed October 21, 2015, http://dictionary.reference.com/browse/dream?s=t.

the pictures, images, and aspirations, He is directing us towards. So the God who never slumbers waits for us to fall asleep. Once we are asleep He introduces a future and a hope He prepared for us prior to conception. Not only does God provide us with dreams, He is willing to assist us in the process of bringing them to fruition. I'll even be bold enough to state if our dream is so small we can accomplish it without Him, it's only a fraction of what He'd like to do through us in our lifetime.

If you find yourself the recipient of a pleasant, wonderful, exciting dream that makes you want to stay asleep or causes you to hit the snooze button to pick up where you left off, it is extremely important you immediately record what you saw, thought, and imagined in your sedation. This is how you capture your dream. Even if you cannot remember all the details, write the main portion of your dream, the portion you earnestly desire or remember most. One useful technique is to nightly stage a notebook, designated for D.R.E.A.M. only, within arm's reach. Ensure you have a writing utensil attached to it so you won't have to fumble around trying to find something to write with. Staging your stationery is important because you may lose details in the shuffle. Exercise discipline to capture dreams consistently so you don't miss out on anything great that comes your way. Just as you've made it a habit to secure your home or automobile by locking the doors, secure your dreams by locking them into the notepad by your sleeping area.

Now you know how to capture your dream, let's revisit the quote from the beginning of this chapter and expound upon what the wise man meant when he offered the pithy saying.

Hope deferred makes the heart sick:

In your journey towards achieving your dream you will navigate through unfamiliar times in life. It may seem there is no limit to how long you'll remain where you are. In spite of your efforts to advance you find yourself in the same place you were the day prior. As you draw closer to what you believe will happen it may appear the thing you desire is moving further away. This deferment brings about a weakening of the will. It compels most people to cancel their lengthy uncomfortable journey through the unknown and go back to the quick comfortable familiar. Why do we stop, if we know the dream at the end is worth the effort, why do we give up? The answer is above. Many people who start with energy do not have the strength to sustain the belief they once had in the beginning of their journey. The drawn out process of waiting leaves them in a weakened state, causing them to cease their quest towards their endeavor.

*Note: If you find yourself here, be encouraged! Rather than turning back, keep in mind, the majority of successful people pushed through and continued the journey. In these moments you must be consistent, insistent, and persistent. Open your heart to the inspiration of others who have been in similar situations and overcome to realize their dreams. Also look for ways to contribute to the success of those around you, the experience of progression provides you hope to press forward.

A dream fulfilled is a tree of life:

Part 2 of this passage provides us the answer to what we need to sustain our forward progress. A dream fulfilled is a tree of life. Notice the quote given says "a dream fulfilled". A dream can be yours or someone else's. Too often we get upset when someone else's dream comes to pass while we've been laboring and waiting on ours.

We may feel as if there is a quota on realized dreams and their accomplishment impedes our progress. Your choice to hate or congratulate someone else in their dream expression or realization makes a significant difference in your life.

It is important to rejoice with others as they share their realized dreams because then we get to taste the fruit of life that flourishes from them. This fruit gives us inspirational energy to progress forward and continue where most people would stop due to malnourishment. Dreams, whether yours or someone else's are so powerful even if they are not fully realized at the moment, can resonate and motivate others to help you as you share it. Think about Dr. Martin Luther King Jr. and his famous dream, how it provided inspiration for people in his day and generations to come. Your God given dream is just as significant and powerful! Most people go to sleep to dream, now it's time to wake up and live yours.

A dream fulfilled is a tree of life:

Part 2 of this passage provides us the answer to what we need to sustain our forward progress. A dream fulfilled is a tree of life. Notice the quote given says "a dream fulfilled". A dream can be yours or someone else's. Too often we get upset when someone else's dream comes to pass while we've been laboring and waiting on ours.

We may feel as if there is a quota on realized dreams and their accomplishment impedes our progress. Your choice to hate or congratulate someone else in their dream expression or realization makes a significant difference in your life.

It is important to rejoice with others as they share their realized dreams because then we get to taste the fruit of life that flourishes from them. This fruit gives us inspirational energy to progress forward and continue where most people would stop due to malnourishment. Dreams, whether yours or someone else's are so powerful even if they are not fully realized at the moment, can resonate and motivate others to help you as you share it. Think about Dr. Martin Luther King Jr. and his famous dream, how it provided inspiration for people in his day and generations to come. Your God given dream is just as significant and powerful! Most people go to sleep to dream, now it's time to wake up and live yours.

DREAM

#1
DREAM
(FOUNDATION)

*Capture your dreams, they lay the foundation
for your vision.*

CHAPTER TWO

Vision

"You've got to See it before you see it, or you never will see it!"

- Karen Clark-Sheard

Though a dream is synonymous with a vision the two are not the same. A common mistake is interchanging the terms, which dilutes the effect of D.R.E.A.M. Dreams occur when we sleep, we may not have active control over them, and if we don't focus on what we dreamt about it will escape us. According to dictionary.com a vision is "1. sight or 2. an experience in which a personage, thing, or event appears vividly or credibly to the mind, although not actually present, often under the influence of a divine or other agency".[4] Considering the two definitions of vision, one may truly appreciate Karen Clark-Sheard's quote because it

---

[4] dictionary,"" dictionary.com, accessed October 21, 2015, http://dictionary.reference.com/browse/vision?s=t.

illustrates the two meanings of vision while delineating physical sight from imagination. In this chapter we'll explore the second definition which describes what we envision or see in our mind. Simply defined, a vision is a vivid description of your future as you see it in the eyes of your imagination. By developing a vision based off of the dream you captured, you maintain the focus and consistency to keep your life oriented toward your dreams. You may now take your captured dream and cultivate it with the deliberate use of your imagination and D.R.E.A.M. stationery.

To place further emphasis on the importance of vision is the truth, "where there is no vision people cast off restraint".[5] If you do not keep your vision in front of you when setting goals, making plans, and executing your plans, eventually you will lose sight of where you're headed and why you're going. Losing sight of your vision makes it easy to be careless in your pursuits and ultimately give up on what you saw. Keep you

---

[5] biblegateway,"" biblegateway.com, accessed October 21, 2015,
https://www.biblegateway.com/passage/?search=proverbs+29%3A18&version=AMP

vision in front of you at all times!

Cast your vision on paper and consider, it doesn't cost any more money or resources to envision something big over something small. Life's experiences and disappointments have conditioned us to manage our expectations for our envisioned outcomes. We've learned how to budget our visions, keeping them limited to what we or someone close to us has already done. What we currently have, or what we think we can do in our present state and current ability should never influence our vision. A common mistake we make is limiting our vision in the imaginary realm to what we presently have in the physical realm.

If you have ever been a part of a hypothetical lottery conversation, think of how lavish we are when imagining our outcome. We acknowledge the odds but in the moment we explain what we'd do, it becomes real to us. Sometimes it's enough for us to take action and purchase a ticket. If you learn how to exceed your self-induced limits you won't need to hit the lottery and you will identify what money can't provide and obtain that as well!

I acknowledge the present in which we live has limits imposed by life's situations, but our imagination only has the limits we assign to it. No one has authority over what you are permitted to imagine. You are the captain of your mind! Do not sell yourself short of what you can actually accomplish by limiting your vision to what you currently see. Most people are subject to what they see, but people who accomplish their dreams understand what they see is subject to what they believe! Our potential is not what we have already done but what we have yet to do; therefore, as long as you're alive your potential has no limits. If we are not careful we will set limits for ourselves because we refused to unbridle our imagination.

Keeping these things in mind, write your vision, make it colorful, detailed and deliberate. Draw pictures and diagrams if you must. Make it so descriptive it brings elation to your heart when you look at it. If a stranger read it they should be able to see what you saw in your mind as you imagined it. Craft it in such a way it fuels excitement and anticipation, motivating you to the next step in D.R.E.A.M. to make it happen.

Warning!: If you do not take time to capture your dream and write what you envision, you will not take time to make it happen. Don't be deceived by the "Got it in my head." trap. That mind set is procrastination rooted in laziness, it will stomp out any chance you have of making your vision real enough to live in. If you do not exercise the discipline to write, you will not exercise the discipline to set your goals, plan to accomplish them, and work your plan to make it happen. Do it now! Like a master of ceremonies (MC) controls the tempo and tone of an event, you control the tempo and tone of your life. Be a T.I.M.E.M.C., one who Takes Initiative Making Every Moment Count.

DREAM

VISION

#2
VISION
(IMAGINATION)

Use your imagination to cultivate your dreams,
See (imagine) it before you see it (with your eyes).

CHAPTER THREE

Goals

"If you don't know where you're going any road will get you there."

- Lewis Carroll

Next in the steps toward accomplishing your dreams is setting goals in line with your vision. In this chapter we'll delve into what goals are and why you must set them to see your vision in reality.

Goals are "the result or achievement toward which effort is directed; aim; end".[6] Even further a goal can be labeled as a milestone, objective, definitive aim, something to strive for. It is paramount you set your goals in alignment with your vision. Nesting your goals in this manner will set the conditions for manifesting your vision as you imagined it. Each goal accomplished brings you closer to your envisioned

---

[6] dictionary,"" dictionary.com, accessed October 21, 2015, http://dictionary.reference.com/browse/goal?s=t.

outcome.

In America the majority of people who make resolutions have the same few concerns in common. Each year the Monday after January 1st, a large group of US citizens exercise two of the top three most common themes for a New Year's Resolution: lose weight and have more money. There is something to be said about setting goals. Statistics report those who explicitly make resolutions, set their yearly goals, are 10 times more likely to attain their objectives versus those who do not.[7]

Since losing weight and having more money are two of the most popular resolutions, we'll use these for goal setting examples. Before we jump into caloric deficit and workout regimen or savings and investments, we'll address the big ticket item that fuels our goals, vision. First we'll envision what our ideal weight and build will be (if you have a picture of a body style, now would be a great time to pull it out and

---

[7] Statistic Brain Research Institute,"" statisticbrain.com, accessed October 21, 2015, http://www.statisticbrain.com/new-years-resolution-statistics/.

post it where you can see it multiple times a day; i.e. refrigerator, mirror, etc.). What clothes size and shape would we like to see once we accomplish our physical goals?

Financially, we'll envision what it would be like to have zero debt, an additional three months' salary in savings, and a maxed out retirement fund. Imagine how relaxing it would be after paying utilities each month to have a surplus of income. No more billing statements in the mail or emails concerning the debt we have yet to pay. The usual money that goes to a mortgage, credit card payment, or a looming college loan is now at our disposal to give to our favorite charity, put towards a creative idea, or take the vacation we always wanted. Visions remain the reason why we set our goals, never lose sight of your vision!

The physical and financial vision statement could be:

By December 31st next year, starting from 204lbs and 22% body fat, I see myself 180lbs and 10% body fat going from a 36" waist to a 32" waist in pants (include a favorite picture of the look I'd like to achieve); financially I see three months of salary tucked away in my savings account, my retirement fund is maxed out, and I have zero balance on college loans and credit card debt.

Imagine how it will be at the end of this physical and financial endeavor and keep it in mind. Memorize (lock it in your mind), internalize (set it in your heart), then actualize (achieve it in reality); M.I.A.

One of the best ways to exercise goal setting is by using the acronym, S.M.A.R.T. created by George Doran, Arthur Miller, and James Cunningham in the 1981 November issue of Management Review.[8] In the article they provided an easy to remember way to list goals. S.M.A.R.T. stands for specific, measurable, attainable, realistic, and time bound.

In line with the vision above, our goals could be:

---

[8] Smart Goals Guide,"" www.smart-goals-guide.com, accessed October 21, 2015, http://www.smart-goals-guide.com/smart-goal.html.

Physically: In the next 12 months lose 2lbs and 1% body fat each month, lose 1/3" each month off of my waist.

Financially: In the next 12 months set a budget to save 1/4 of income after taxes each pay period, select a retirement fund and contribute the maximum amount towards retirement monthly, cancel college and credit card debt.

These two examples are general and may even seem oversimplified, if that is your case be more detailed when writing your goals. These simple yet powerful goals pass the S.M.A.R.T. test and are strong enough to connect us to the vision of our ideal physique and financial disposition at the year's end. Our milestones are set. Each month we meet these objectives brings us closer to what we envisioned. At this point the only thing keeping us from where we are now and where we see ourselves in the future is a solid plan to achieve our goals.

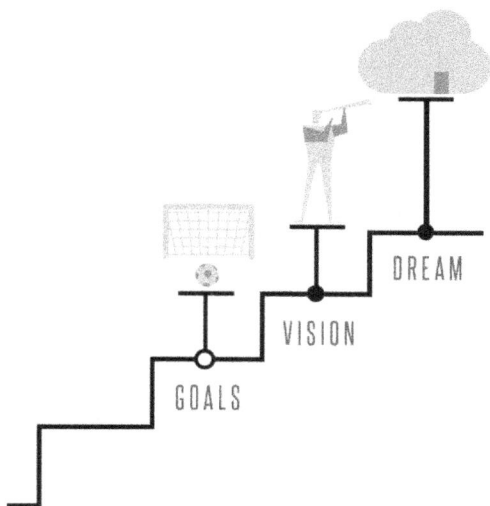

DREAM

VISION

GOALS

#3

GOALS

[MILESTONES]

Set your goals in line with your vision, each goal you accomplish will get you closer to living in what you once imagined.

CHAPTER FOUR

Plan

"He who fails to plan, plans to fail"
- Ben Franklin

The second to last step in this methodical process is planning. Plans are necessary when working to accomplish goals. They keep our effort organized and protect us from jeopardizing our definitive aim.

A plan is "a scheme or method of acting, doing, proceeding, making, etc. developed in advance". [9] Plans provide detailed instruction on actions, timing and resourcing, they spell out the way ahead to achieve your objective.

As we talk about plans, keep in mind they are only as good as the time and effort we put into making and practicing them. This is another place in which

---

[9] dictionary,"" dictionary.com, accessed October 21, 2015, http://dictionary.reference.com/browse/plan?s=t.

consistency plays a major factor in D.R.E.A.M. Devise your plan and stick with it.

"Good planning and hard work lead to prosperity, but hasty shortcuts lead to poverty." [10] Often people talk about what they would like to accomplish, but they fail to devise a good plan to get there. Some have a good plan but apply half of the effort required to execute it well and others barely have a plan and work hard but still fall short of their goals. The combination of good planning and hard work is what we must practice to prosper. People who habitually fail in their pursuits, neglect the balanced combination of good planning and hard work. Continually employing hasty short cuts, they often achieve impoverished results consistently.

A good plan provides a list of steps to follow to include actions taken, timing, and resources. A great plan includes contingencies which provide options moving forward, should you encounter obstacles you

[10] biblegateway,"" biblegateway.com, accessed October 21, 2015,
https://www.biblegateway.com/passage/?search=proverbs+21%3A5&version=NLT

maintain forward progress. You may not be able to predict which obstacles will come, but you can anticipate them and plan accordingly.

Develop contingencies to achieve each goal you set because life has a way of remaining unpredictable. An acronym you may use that includes contingencies for planning and preparation to achieve your goals is P.A.C.E. Originally used for communications planning, P.A.C.E. is a great checklist to apply in our planning and preparation for achievement. P.A.C.E. stands for primary, alternate, contingency, and emergency. [11] Knowing you are prepared for the variable challenges life presents will give you confidence to execute your plan with enthusiasm.

Your primary plan can be described as the straight line approach. Often very simple, it lays out how you will achieve your goal in ideal conditions. We can agree life is not always ideal and our primary plans

---

[11] graywolfsurvival,"" graywolfsurvival.com, accessed October 21, 2015,
http://graywolfsurvival.com/2096/prepping-101-how-to-plan-pace/.

are often challenged but sometimes they work the way we intended without a hitch.

Hopefully things go as we primarily planned, if not we are still moving forward towards achievement because we have an alternate plan. An alternate plan is another common way to achieve your goal with minimal to no significant impact on energy, timing, or resources. You may even incorporate aspects of your alternate plan with the primary.

Should your primary and alternate plans fail or get blocked you may exercise your contingency plan. Contingency plans are less desirable than the first two because they are not as fast or convenient, but they will accomplish the goal in a reasonable amount of time.

The last option in the P.A.C.E. method is emergency planning. Emergency planning is characterized as your last ditch effort. An emergency plan is the most costly option of the four methods. Implementing this plan would have a significant impact on your overall vision. It may even cause a need to go back and reset your goals and start a new line of planning.

To provide further understanding of how one may actualize P.A.C.E. in an everyday life example, we'll use monthly bill paying scenarios. A primary means of paying bills can be with money you earned from your job. As an employee you earn a wage and pay bills from your checking account. An alternate way of financing your life's operations can be from money earned in part time self-employment. The alternate can either take the place of your primary method of paying bills or it may work together with it. A contingency would be exhausting money from your savings account to pay bills. Though you accomplish paying bills, you are exhausting funds you may have stored up for another use. Think of how long it may have taken to amass your savings as opposed to your primary account. In this example the contingency is certainly more costly than the other two options. An emergency means of paying monthly bills could be liquidating your retirement fund. This option results in paying monthly bills at a very costly expense, the expense of your future ability to retire from the workforce.

By now you've caught on that just as our vision is attached to our dream, and our goal is nested in our vision, our plans connect us to accomplishing our goals. At the start of your plan you may include subject matter experts on a strategy (there is safety in a multitude of counsel[12]). Good advice will keep you from wasting energy, effort, and valuable resources. Learn from successful people who have excelled in areas you wish to be successful in. They are qualified to help with setting your goals and laying out your plans.

To place emphasis on the previous statement, ensure you ask people with expertise to help you. Beware of false experts. How can you measure expertise? Certainly you may go by their credentials or recommendations from someone you hold in high esteem. In addition, I recommend you look at the results they yield in their own lives. As you can tell a tree by its fruit, you can determine a person's level of

---

[12] biblegateway,"" biblegateway.com, accessed October 21, 2015,
https://www.biblegateway.com/passage/?search=Proverbs+11:14&version=KJV

expertise by how they apply knowledge and the results they yield.[13]

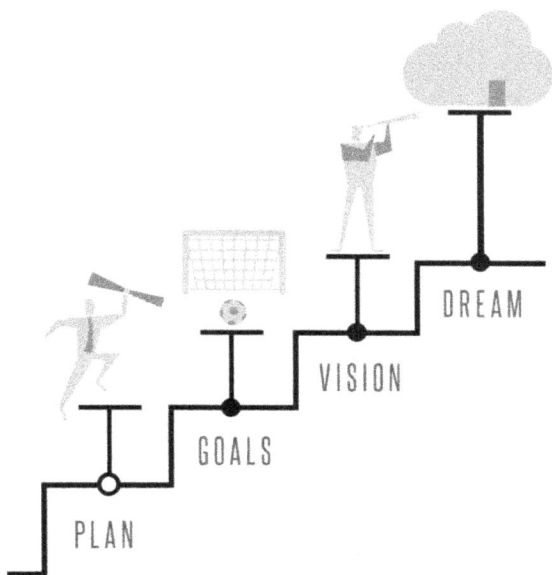

DREAM

VISION

GOALS

PLAN

#4

PLAN
(WAY AHEAD)

*Plan prudently to accomplish your goals,
follow your custom crafted road map to
success daily; make adjustments as needed.*

CHAPTER FIVE

Conclusion

"The best way to predict your future is to create it"
- Abraham Lincoln

If you followed the steps as you completed this book, you've taken the time to put D.R.E.A.M. into action. Now it means more when people throw out a cliché involving dreams. Luck is no longer the main ingredient to seeing your dreams come to pass.

By finishing this book you exhibited the desire to realize your dreams, now multiply the desire by applying the knowledge you've gained from D.R.E.A.M. You now have at your disposal a solid method of connecting your invisible future to the visible present. Refer to it as often as needed. Use this as a reference to deliberately realize your ends (dreams) achieving them methodically. By capturing your dreams, developing your vision, setting your goals, and then planning prudently to accomplish them, you have drastically increased your chances of realizing what you saw while you were sleeping. You are now equipped to manifest your dreams into reality. If people are destroyed for what they don't know or what they know and won't do, they may also prosper by learning and applying D.R.E.A.M. to life. Life is what you make it, make it happen!

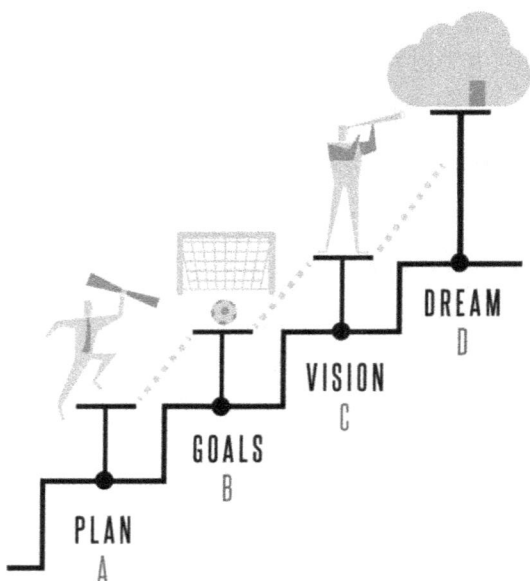

CONCLUSION

Now that you've finished with a detailed plan, ultimately set on the foundation of your dream
A. work hard on executing your plan
B.achieve your goals
C. achieving your goals accomplishes the vision
D.your vision realizes the dream.
Now do it!

Life is what you make it
By Simon Billy Bleuh Flake:

Life is what you make it, so make it happen

It's yours for you to take it, so take action

Don't follow the crowd, follow your passion

If it doesn't exist, create your own fashion

Life requires work, it's up to you to work it

It's yours for you to mold so mold it until it's perfect

Life will be tough, so toughen up

In the midst of destruction never self-destruct

Don't complain about problems, compare the solutions

You go where you look, look for a resolution

Life is about living, live it to the full

Life is about pushing, push life until it pulls

Life is about giving, give life all you've got

Life is about sharing whether you like it or not

If there was ever a time to be involved, now is the time to answer life's call